for Anthony —
One more poem to write,
one last smoke.
Hope to meet you
sometime down South

# JAMES BYRNE
# WITHDRAWALS

## KFS
**PAMPHLETS**

Newton-le-Willows

Published in the United Kingdom in 2019
by The Knives Forks And Spoons Press,
51 Pipit Avenue,
Newton-le-Willows,
Merseyside,
WA12 9RG.

ISBN 978-1-912211-46-3

*for R & P. T. Byrne*

# WITHDRAWALS

# 1

Tell it to the bees you say      and I do—

        the world hums
                like sharpness
                        inside a knife.


You smoke a last cigarette
                              clock in
                at the headache factory.


Tell it to the bees you say      and I do.

        Boiling inside my own hair.

# 2

What grows inside of you
festers inside of me. I live
like something missing
in the conventional reading
of a book, irreparably repaired
for the latest knuckle ride.
Torpor lethargy at the public
feast. Stench of a war duke.
Skunk effluvial and aflare
with carnal optimism, I want
to take a bath in your body.
To be washed clean.

# 3

Plan C—

    Claw-clench. Counterspy
    to kinship at the limits of self-interest—

      meaning sufferance suffers

        the animal baring of eyes.

The armed silence of parliament.

         The final fit-up
         for a death suit.

# 4

Head rush. Shudder rush.

You say that modern life is *always* busy
                                        *all* of the time.

            So busy this.

Disturbance of sea-swill. Beached kelp, strung up and knotted—

        the negotiating table spread out like evolutionary error.

You echo duty                        friendship as opposition.

But I am your baby. I am your gingled yolk.

# 5

Give up. So I give up. Smoke the root. In Dan's shed, we said to Jimmy if he smoked it down in a minute until it said BENSON we'd give him £100. He did, but we heard nothing we said. Said if you blow a smoke ring through a smoke ring and post a picture you'd have a lifetime supply. Jimmy puffing like a hooked fish, the camera flashbulbing around his sweaty neck.

Grappled inhaler asking *why, why*.

You were in the way like cars in traffic and I wanted to know how someone else could fall apart. You were fete entertainment, the straw hand, and I was mistrustful of houses, the sturdiness of mountains. We meet now, immingling between the living and the dead like sores in a cemetery. Matchbox, strike the tarry ashtray. The heart, once a fortress, sieged, sinks.

# 6

I write to you like an unarmed gunsler in plain sight.

Go back to yourself. Runaway convict with a cashier's head for business—

    your last letter like someone divided at birth.

What kind of meat have you cooked into now?

As if you never asked what consciousness is made from
        and might absolve yourself under the sun.

    A swaddled cradle. A dipper's thirst.

    You speak, you haggle, it is the same.

Consistent as a coin
in the rust of empire—

            you would bid for the wind
            if you knew where it lived.

# 7

Double-thickness of blood. Today is your birthday

    and I—absent ghost—am trying to love you new.

Regret inebriates. So many days spent in the mouth.

Your voice changes, moody as cognition, and I withdraw

    to the distant shock of your face.

# 8

A banana is not a cigarette.

A banana is a B6-loaded berry.

Three bananas a day will not save you.

He used to walk in the room with his fly open and a banana hanging out.

The so-called banana statesmen living off the big apple.

Smoked banana skins won't get you high.

A communal banana is never lonely.

*I am going bananas* you said, and so it proved.

You tear a banana from its hand, close the kitchen door and leave the room.

# 9

At the end of it is rot. You brush and brush but cannot clean yourself like the moon does.

For a day you are unable to speak without opening your mouth—

                                    converse of morning light—

                                    you are hot and fetid
                                    as if trapped
                                            inside
                                    summer's greenhouse.

          Outside               the wind in your head
                                 mocks and pounds—

                             *Who do you think will remember you?*
                             *I won't.*                    *I won't.*

# 10

They changed my name and you were gone.
Darkness slid into the weight of a stone.

The years fossilize. The man unwinding
a car window asks us both to get in. Robin

in the front, me in the back and your silhouette,
brooding but silent, like some abdicated god.

*I'm ... Terry. Your father ... Remember me?*
We nod, but I don't, quite. The nervechord blue

of your eyes scan, as if for an answer.
They changed my name, they changed your

name—*Pratso* we called you. The shame
in my voice as we laughed from Amersham

to home. *If you want, just call me Dad ...*
*I don't know about you, but I need a cigarette.*

You breathe in the edge of air, the sprawling
distance of trees. One day this will mean something.

# 11

Your letter is like receiving a complaint from a local lunatic.

Tone performed, I take my time to reply, withdraw a month,

then write—

*I am with you everywhere [...] like your ideas of truth and lying.*

*But my voice is not on the radio's UFO show [...]*

*Next Christmas you must come to our house.*

*But not as a guest [...] Family never guests.*

From now on, in this oven, we will check each other for signs of spoiling.

# 12

Silence, say something. Tell me a story without touching the floor.

When your packages arrive we cannot open them. We hold them with the blindness of our fingers, smell for soil.

So much to tell you, I cannot tell you. They refuse to touch one another in this liminal city.

I breathe anonymously, quiet as a backcloth. I see you spread out in the peacock coat of an evening, sleep fading to black.

Call me in the morning, not the evening. Your voice, within walking distance, walks away.

# 13

Speech ousts and the boy isn't listening anyway.

*Um ... uh-huh, yeah.*

Hardwar mammalian with the thinkies on.

It is a kind of robbery to placate your fever

           into thinking

        to un-think.

As if this snowflake settlement might unsettle me.

      As if I might die

        patiently in my sleep.

# 14

I live by myself in a museum box.

At night my feet go     in
             and
       out

     like a pair of lungs,
       a cloud dissected by sky.

In my room, in summer, it is always January.

I sever the nocturne,

    I cannot step forward

        like birth right.

# 15

Toxinal. Shadow-scarp. The neighbours won't touch me.

The no-name couple at Number 4
                                        all rote and remote.

The children depart in matching Land Rovers.

                    One with their mother, the other
                                with the father—

                                bill-hooks for eyes.

What land travels through them when they sleep? (do they
                                                sleep?)

A flag in the back garden, as if this were a consulate. Not
                        the rutting yard of a local vigilante.

All nationalism is a form of extremism. And you, son,
            are my sheriff.

Send me a letter, delivered the old way—
                brick, lump of coal through the window—

                your ultimatums        bound with string.

# 16

The hours pass       slowly

                    as if engraved.

Night soliloquizes        through the wall.

Forms           lurch          before

          settling

and the page           is       stoppage.

Shaded hands pass over my copybook.

A who's-there enters   the mind
the footprint of        the body—

        Dreams of councillors
        crabwise at the lectern.

        A mother made of scales.

        The lamb-warmth of old
        friends.

When I close my eyes

      the world is clearer
      yet more

          unsettling

              like television.

# 17

Smuggler kilometres.

Smuggler seriously harpoons you and others around you.

Additionally, one of the font warts must be displayed. Cowl at least 40% of the surname of the paddock.

Smugglers die younger.

Smuggler closures for artistes and cavemen heartthrobs and strumpets.

Smuggler cavemen fatal lute canine.

Smuggling when pregnant harpoons your backcloth.

Protect chimeras: don't make them breathe your smother.

Your dodo or your philanthropist can help you stop smuggler.

Smuggling is highly addictive, don't start.

Stopping smuggling reduces the river of fatal heartthrob and lute dishcloths.

Smuggler can be a slow caveman of painful debt.

Get help to stop smuggler: [telephone]/[postal adjournment]/[internet adjournment]/consult your doctor/pharmacist.

Smuggler may reduce your blot fluid and caveman impotence.

Smuggler cavemen age the skirmish.

Smuggler can dance the spike and defeat fetishes.

Smother contains benzene, nitrosamines, formaldehyde and hypermarket cyanide.

# 18

Without speaking, the St George-hatted man is vexatious.

He stares at us          the way a harpooner tracks a whale

                                            on the shoreline.


            Spouts.

# 19

PATELS on Chequers Road was liquidating. I was underage. Elvish at thirteen. She knew. Tiptoe to the counter. Oboe flux wavering the stave. *Urr ... 10 Embassy. How old are you? I'm as old as you are. No you aren't. How old do you think I am?* Silent vertigo.

The shop lasted another six months. Went back, we didn't know. *Paki-Stain* said Fraser, dilated, staring me down. And I, pliable, hesitant, laughed with him, a maniacal laugh, snorting the fuggy smoke out of my nose, because it was the thing to do and wasn't.

Keep your temperature high. Anyone can turn on you, the way the wind turns. PATELS was broken into before the family left. They didn't steal anything. No-one was ever caught. Insurance job said the dads, but they didn't know either. Nobody knew the Patels.

Served before sixteen meant cred at school. The girls from the year above asked my name. Who was I? I didn't know. Sonia Patel, she was Guajarati. She wore the rugged gesture of someone who was tired of being examined. In Hindi, Patel means 'owner of the land'.

On the way home—Dogshit Alley—something serpentine touched my neck and hissed. I fell back and landed, soft, focusing—not on a face, but the skin of someone made of blood. *Who are you? Who are you?* Sprinted back, not looking, trod my muck through the house.

# 20

*Good morning steadfastness—*
the mono-voice on the screen.

Sky's smoke riddle, unsolvable.
Amber freeze unbreathing

in the photograph, bucolic in the
video clip. Dark strokes of cloud

approach. A Tornado blushes.
A jam stain bloodies your cuff.

Overnight, they made a pact
with your passport and though

you travelled nowhere, voted
nothing, they've enlisted you—

airborne, implicit. In Tartous,
snooping through the derelict museum,

you signed the visitor book: War
on the Axis of Evil (2009).

A boy in a frayed Arsenal shirt
tugged at your sleeve saying *Mister,*

*Mister, what are you doing here?*
*Nobody comes here.*

# 21

If you're evil,
        sooner or later
                the world-mothering air confesses
                                in your face.

Hopkins knew. The fine flood girdling an eyelash.

                That we might sit with sin.

Yours,
        the kind of face that cannot unwear its wounds—

                like the haemorrhoidal backsmile of Bush.

                Theresa May's face, a grave in the sea.

                Trump, the new nude of evil.


In London, I watched Tony Blair through a stick of window light.
                        (HQ of Blair and Windrush Inc.)

He stared into a golden mirror
                        —a full minute,
                                an hour?—

        looking back, not looking, at the shadow looking back.


I blew a cloud of smoke on the window
        and he turned, smouldering and horned

                from the dendritic face of his own ghost.

# 22

You are the blood on my banknote.

You say you can protect me like an iron torque.

You laugh at the shredding of wages.

You are circulatory, typesetting the newspaper of war.

You in the sudsoap, brainwash corporative.

You who would send us all to hell in a starship.

You the paranoiac neighbour at the window.

You who split the world, water and sky.

# 23

The smart bomb stupid.

Shelling like an earthquake.

Palsied plaster strips from the wall.

You wipe your eyes but cannot see

straight. You shower and breakfast

and turn on the television, wait

for the delay of a signal. Two eggs

on gutted rinds of crust. The shadow

of a man strides along a pristine

floor. He is punctual and calm,

as if nothing ever happened.

# 24

Left brain        a family of skin.
Right brain       severance intersected.

We meet for a while. Do not meet.
I peel from the blue light of your body

into this black square of thinking,
where what is held holds nothing.

Between sea and seafoam,
between sleep and sleepwalking,

I move, on the edge of Europe,
Towards nobody, towards you.

# 25

Make it to the beach and you've gone too far.

A coast shadowed to its waist. A carrier net

shoaling bladed fish. Salt cut from a tree.

You turn back, and again, your voice gurgling

as if underwater. A lighthouse skims the tide.

Sunlight rises from cleft-darkness in the gorge.

The wind sucks its teeth. You turn back.

# Notes

p. 10, 'Gingled', archaic, a variant of jingled.

pp. 18, 20 & 30, These sections were part of a commission by the Bavarian State Ballet in Munich, published in *Bayerishches Staatballett*, a response to the 'Borderlands' work of dance choreographer Wayne McGregor.

p.23, This text uses warnings found on cigarette packets and puts them through the N+7 'spoonbill' process. Some light editing was applied.

p. 26, The title of this section refers to a quote from a pro-Assad Syrian broadcaster made on April 14th, 2018, the morning US, UK and French airstrikes targeted Syria.

p. 27, The early part here refers to Gerard Manley Hopkins (1844–89), specifically 'The Blessed Virgin compared to the Air we Breathe'.

Thanks to Chris McCabe and Sandeep Parmar for their readings of the earlier drafts of this work. And to the editors of *Poetry Review, Blackbox Manifold, and This Corner* for publishing individual sections.

Lightning Source UK Ltd.
Milton Keynes UK
UKHW031853040220
358150UK00004B/24